W9-BMV-280

Withdrawn

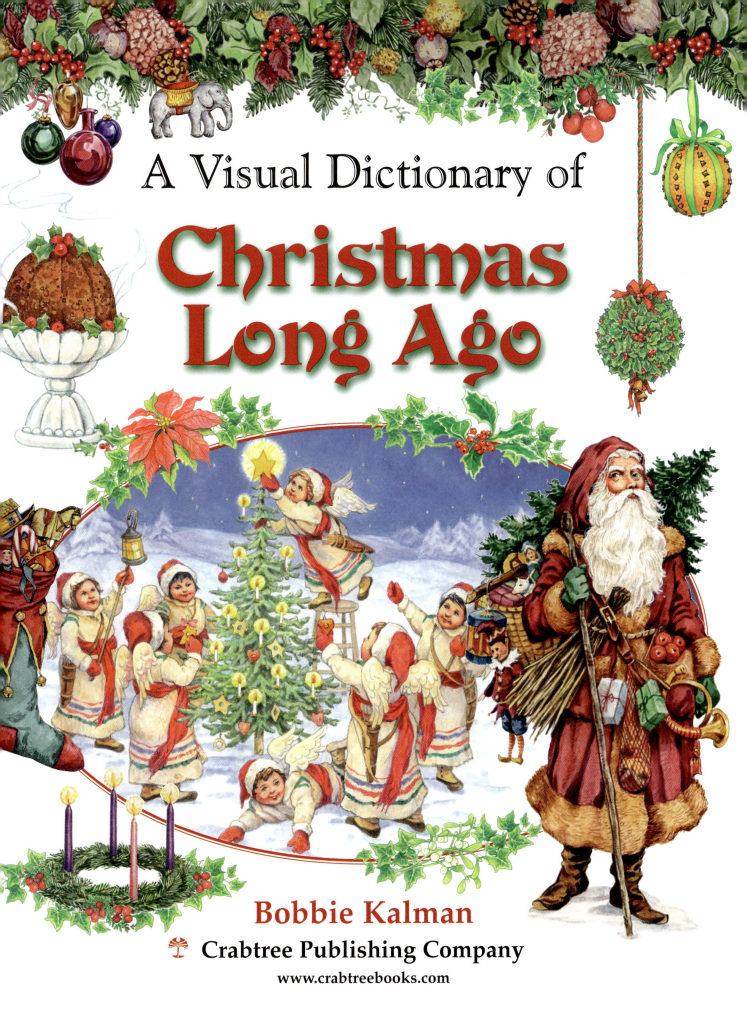

A Visual Dictionary of

Christmas Long Ago

Bobbie Kalman

Crabtree Publishing Company

www.crabtreebooks.com

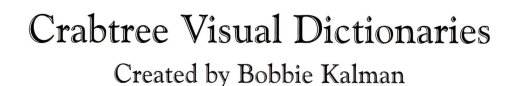

Crabtree Visual Dictionaries
Created by Bobbie Kalman

For my cousin Benedek Varga,
who made the Christmas of 2010 truly memorable.
Boldog Karácsonyi emlékkel és szeretettel

Author and Editor-in-Chief
Bobbie Kalman

Research
Enlynne Paterson

Editors
Kathy Middleton
Crystal Sikkens

Design
Bobbie Kalman
Katherine Berti

Print and production coordinator
Katherine Berti

Prepress technician
Katherine Berti

Illustrations
Illustrations by Barbara Bedell except:
Antoinette "Cookie" Bortolon: page 14 (bottom)
Bonna Rouse: page 14 (tree-top left and right)

Photographs and reproductions
Circa Art: pages 6 (bottom), 7 (bottom),
  12 (bottom), 13 (bottom), 20 (top right
  and bottom), 24 (bottom), 25 (middle left
  and bottom right)
Harpers Weekly: page 26 (bottom)
Shutterstock: front cover (santas, angel, and
  children with yule log), back cover (bottom
  right), pages 4 (bottom), 8 (bottom), 9 (bottom
  right), 10 (top), 14 (top), 16 (bottom), 17 (top
  left), 24 (top left and right), 25 (bottom left and
  middle), 26 (top right), 27, 31 (bottom)

Library and Archives Canada Cataloguing in Publication

Kalman, Bobbie, 1947-
   A visual dictionary of Christmas long ago / Bobbie Kalman.

(Crabtree visual dictionaries)
Includes index.
Issued also in electronic format.
ISBN 978-0-7787-3506-9 (bound).--ISBN 978-0-7787-3526-7 (pbk.)

   1. Christmas--Dictionaries, Juvenile. 2. Christmas--Pictorial
works--Juvenile literature. 3. Picture dictionaries--Juvenile literature.
I. Title. II. Series: Kalman, Bobbie, 1947- . Crabtree visual dictionaries.

GT4985.K349 2011   j394.266303   C2011-900070-9

Library of Congress Cataloging-in-Publication Data

Kalman, Bobbie.
   A visual dictionary of Christmas long ago / Bobbie Kalman.
      p. cm. -- (Crabtree visual dictionaries)
   Includes index.
   ISBN 978-0-7787-3526-7 (pbk. : alk. paper) --
   ISBN 978-0-7787-3506-9 (reinforced library binding : alk. paper) -
- ISBN 978-1-4271-9474-9 (electronic pdf : alk. paper)
   1. Christmas--Dictionaries. I. Title. II. Series.

GT4985.K18 2011
394.2663'03--dc22
                                                        2010052193

Crabtree Publishing Company
www.crabtreebooks.com   1-800-387-7650

Printed in the U.S.A./022011/CJ20101228

Published in Canada
Crabtree Publishing
616 Welland Ave.
St. Catharines, Ontario
L2M 5V6

Published in the United States
Crabtree Publishing
PMB 59051
350 Fifth Avenue, 59th Floor
New York, New York 10118

Published in the United Kingdom
Crabtree Publishing
Maritime House
Basin Road North, Hove
BN41 1WR

Published in Australia
Crabtree Publishing
386 Mt. Alexander Rd.
Ascot Vale (Melbourne)
VIC 3032

Contents

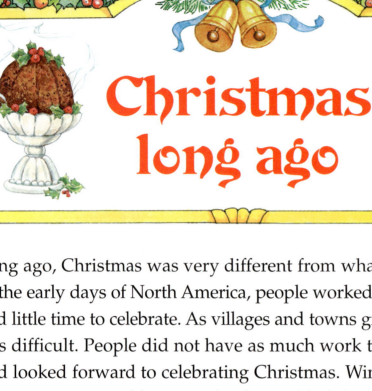

Christmas long ago

Long ago, Christmas was very different from what it is today. In the early days of North America, people worked very hard and had little time to celebrate. As villages and towns grew, life became less difficult. People did not have as much work to do in winter and looked forward to celebrating Christmas. Winter was also an easier time to travel because sleighs could glide over snow, even where there were no roads. People enjoyed being outdoors. They went for sleigh rides on the snow and skated on ice. People visited one another and had parties. They danced, played games, and told stories. Christmas was even a popular time for weddings!

Christmas activities

Find out more about the Christmas activities shown in the
pictures below by turning to the pages listed next to each picture.

*Christmas
sleigh rides
or hayrides
(page 12)*

*Christmas
stockings
(pages
18, 23)*

*(center)
going to
church
(page 13)*

*ghost
stories
(pages
10, 12)*

*Christmas
parties and
weddings
(pages 10–11,
28–29)*

The story of Christmas

Christmas celebrates the birth of Jesus Christ. Christians believe that Jesus is the son of God. Jesus was born in a town called Bethlehem more than 2,000 years ago. Bethlehem is in present-day Israel. Jesus was born into a Jewish family to parents named Mary and Joseph.

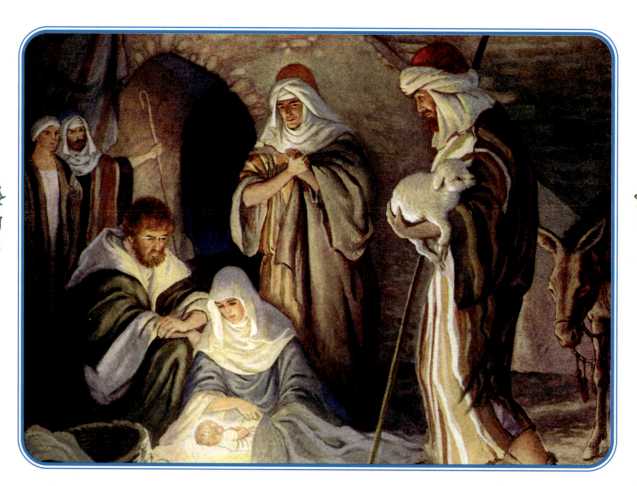

Shepherds saw a bright star and an angel in the sky that led them to Jesus (see page 24).

Born in a stable

The land where the parents of Jesus lived was ruled by Romans at that time. The Roman ruler ordered everyone to return to the towns where they were born to be counted and to pay taxes. Joseph and Mary had to travel to Bethlehem. When they arrived, the town was full of travelers, and there were no rooms left for sleeping. A kind man offered Mary and Joseph a **stable** so they would have a roof over their heads. That night, Jesus was born. He was born in a **manger**.

A stable is where animals are kept. A manger is a feed box for cows and sheep.

When Jesus was born, a bright star led Three Kings, also known as Wise Men or Magi, to the stable. The kings brought him gifts. Gifts are given at Christmas to celebrate the birth of Jesus.

Decorating the home

Before there were Christmas trees, people used what they could find outdoors to make their homes look and smell wonderful. Plants like holly, ivy, mistletoe, cranberries, and branches of pine trees were gathered and brought indoors to decorate homes for Christmas. People made beautiful **garlands** and **wreaths** using these natural decorations. They also made decorations using fruit, nuts, candles, and spices such as cinnamon and cloves.

These children are gathering holly. Holly has beautiful red berries.

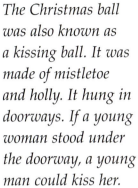

Christmas garlands were hung around doorways and fireplace mantels. Garlands were made by tying together branches and adding apples, cones, nuts, holly, and bows.

The Christmas ball was also known as a kissing ball. It was made of mistletoe and holly. It hung in doorways. If a young woman stood under the doorway, a young man could kiss her.

The Christmas rose blooms in December and made a beautiful Christmas decoration.

Pine branches and cones made a home smell like the outdoors.

Nuts and apples were used as decorations as well as snacks.

Pomanders made a house smell wonderful! Children could make them by sticking cloves into oranges.

Cranberries look like holly. They were used to decorate homes and were eaten with turkey.

The poinsettia plant was brought to the United States from Mexico by Joel Poinsett in the 1800s.

The **Advent** wreath held four candles to mark the four weeks before Christmas. The candles stood for hope, love, joy, and peace. A new candle was lit each week. The pink candle was lit on the third week, representing the joy that Christmas was almost here.

These children are dragging home a special log that will be added to the fire on Christmas Eve. They hope it will be big enough to burn until Christmas Day. What is left of the log will be saved and used to light the fresh Yule log on the next Christmas Eve. The Yule log tradition celebrates Christmas and is believed to bring good health and luck.

Ghost stories and games

People spent the weeks before Christmas celebrating the season with neighbors and friends. They looked forward to Christmas parties, which usually meant lots of food and fun games! Ghost stories were another popular Christmas activity. People sat around a flickering fire telling scary tales. A favorite ghost story was "A Christmas Carol" by Charles Dickens.

Pinch, No Smiling was a game of self-control. One by one, each player turns to a neighbor and pinches his or her nose. The first player to smile or laugh has to pay a **forfeit**, *or penalty, such as a favorite toy. To get a forfeit back, a player has to perform a silly trick, such as hopping around the room on one foot.*

The Cobweb Game was popular at Christmas parties. A spider made of wire hung from the ceiling. Long pieces of string or ribbon—one for each player— were attached to the spider and then wound around the room in a tangled web. The object of the game was to follow one piece of string from the spider to the end, where a Christmas present was waiting.

In the Bag and Stick game, a paper bag filled with treats is hung from the ceiling. One child is blindfolded, spun around, and given a stick. If the first child cannot break open the bag, another child is given a chance. When the bag is finally broken, everyone scrambles to grab as many treats as he or she can!

Games such as Charades tested a child's ability to pretend and act. Guess which animal this boy is pretending to be.

Christmas Eve

Christmas Eve was a busy and exciting time. People often played charades, sang and danced to music played on the piano, or listened to someone read a Christmas tale or tell a ghost story. Children performed Christmas plays that they had spent hours rehearsing. If there was snow, people went for sleigh rides. Sleighs could glide easily over snow, and people enjoyed being outdoors. The air was filled with the music of jingling bells, which were attached to the sleighs and the straps of horses. In the country, people went for hayrides. A wagon filled with hay drove slowly, as its passengers sipped hot apple cider and sang Christmas carols.

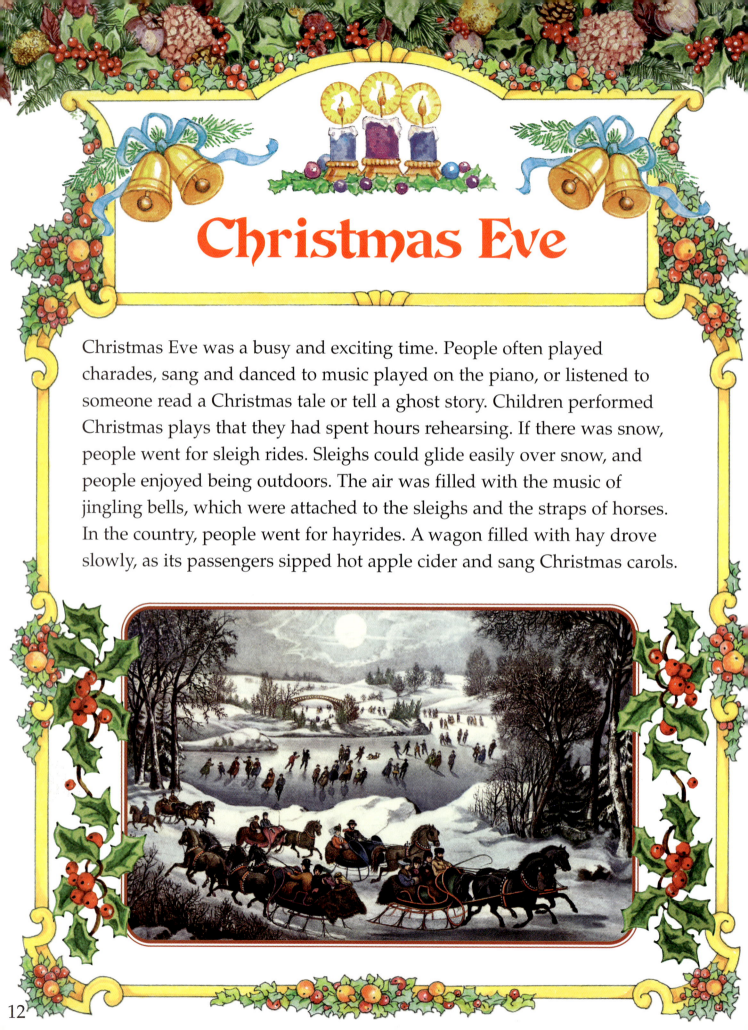

Special church services were held on Christmas Eve and Christmas Day. People wore their best clothes to celebrate the birth of Jesus.

People sang Christmas carols in church. They also sang outside churches and homes. Carolers received food and drinks.

Visiting relatives and friends was a big part of Christmas. Friends organized visiting parties, at which a group of people surprised a family with food, gifts, and music.

The custom of placing candles in windows during Christmastime started in Ireland. The candles were lit on Christmas Eve and burned until January 6. This boy is lighting a candle on Christmas Eve.

13

The Christmas tree

Legend has it that the first Christmas tree was decorated by **Martin Luther** in Germany. One Christmas Eve, Martin Luther went for a walk in the forest. Looking up, he noticed the stars twinkling around the snow-covered treetops, and the sight filled him with wonder. He brought a fir tree home to his family and put candles on its branches. The candles shone like stars.

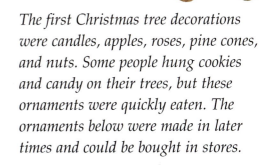

The first Christmas tree decorations were candles, apples, roses, pine cones, and nuts. Some people hung cookies and candy on their trees, but these ornaments were quickly eaten. The ornaments below were made in later times and could be bought in stores.

Queen Victoria's husband, Prince Albert, brought the custom of decorating a Christmas tree from his homeland, Germany, to England. People in North America quickly adopted this custom.

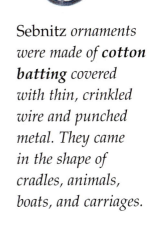

Sebnitz *ornaments were made of* **cotton batting** *covered with thin, crinkled wire and punched metal. They came in the shape of cradles, animals, boats, and carriages.*

Dresdens *were ornaments that looked like metal but were actually made of cardboard. The cardboard was painted silver, gold, or copper.*

German-made blown-glass balls, called kugels, *were among the first Christmas ornaments to be sold in North American shops.*

Cornucopias *were shaped like cones and held candies, fruit, and nuts.*

Gifts for children

In some countries, children receive gifts from Saint Nicholas on December 6, from the Christ Child and angels on Christmas Eve, and from the Three Kings or a grandmother on January 6. Some of these gift-bringers also bring and decorate a Christmas tree in each home. When people came to North America from different countries, they brought their Christmas customs with them. Do you celebrate Christmas? What special Christmas customs and traditions does your family have?

In some places, Santa Claus is also called St. Nicholas, Kriss Kringle, or Father Christmas. He brings gifts to children at Christmastime.

In some European countries, the Christmas tree and gifts are brought by angels on Christmas Eve.

When Jesus was born, Three Kings brought him gifts. The names of the kings are Balthasar, Melchior, and Caspar. Spanish children receive gifts from the Three Kings on January 6.

In some countries, a story is told about a grandmother who searches each house for the baby Jesus so she can bring him gifts. She is still searching for him, so she leaves gifts behind for children instead. In Russia, she is named Babushka. In Italy, people call her Befana.

Who was Saint Nicholas?

Saint Nicholas, or St. Nicholas, was a bishop who lived long ago in a country that is now Turkey. He is called by different names, such as Sinter Klaas, Père Nöel, and Father Christmas. St. Nicholas wore a long coat and rode a horse. In some countries, children believed that he rode a goat! Many people around the world wait for St. Nicholas to come, even though they may not agree on his name, how he looks, where he lives, how he travels, or when he brings gifts.

St. Nicholas helped poor children by filling their boots with gifts while they slept. On the night of December 5, many children around the world put out boots for St. Nicholas to fill. In some places, the boots have been replaced by stockings hung up over the fireplace on Christmas Eve.

German, Austrian, and many European people believe that the Christ Child sends a messenger on Christmas Eve. The messenger appears as an angel in a white robe, bearing gifts and a tree. The angel is called "Christkind," which means "Christ Child" in German. The name Kriss Kringle came from this name.

The people of Finland, Sweden, and some in England, believed that Father Christmas rode a goat called a Yule Goat.

In Russia, St. Nicholas brought food and other gifts to people on the night before December 6.

Père Nöel is the French name of Father Christmas.

A visit from St. Nicholas

In 1823 in North America, Clement Moore changed the way people thought of St. Nicholas. In his poem "A Visit from St. Nicholas," which is now called "Twas the Night Before Christmas," St. Nicholas is described as a jolly old elf with a white beard and a round belly. An artist named Thomas Nast drew pictures for the poem. This St. Nicholas soon became known as "Santa Claus." Santa Claus lives at the North Pole and flies around the world on Christmas Eve with the help of his eight reindeer. Parts of Moore's poem that describe Santa are on the next page.

Thomas Moore described Santa Claus in his poem "A Visit from St. Nicholas." Read part of his poem that talks about how Santa looked.

He was dressed all in fur, from his head to his foot,
And his clothes were all tarnished with ashes and soot.
A bundle of toys he had flung on his back,
And he looked like a peddler, just opening his pack.

His eyes, how they twinkled! His dimples, how merry!
His cheeks were like roses, his nose like a cherry!
His droll little mouth was drawn up like a bow,
And the beard of his chin was as white as the snow...
He had a broad face and a little round belly,
That shook when he laughed, like a bowlful of jelly!
He was chubby and plump, a right jolly old elf,
And I laughed when I saw him, in spite of myself!
A wink of his eye and a twist of his head,
Soon gave me to know I had nothing to dread.

He spoke not a word, but went straight to his work,
And filled all the stockings, then turned with a jerk.
And laying his finger aside of his nose,
And giving a nod, up the chimney he rose!
He sprang to his sleigh, to his team gave a whistle,
And away they all flew like the down of a thistle.
But I heard him exclaim, 'ere he drove out of sight,
"Happy Christmas to all, and to all a good-night!"

Santa's workshop

Santa needs a lot of help to make gifts for all the boys and girls in the world! In Santa's workshop at the North Pole, hundreds of elves work year-round to help him make toys. They work very hard sawing, hammering, painting, and wrapping. On Christmas Eve, they load the toys into Santa's sleigh.

Santa has just 24 hours to deliver toys and fill the Christmas stockings of girls and boys around the world. Flying reindeer pull Santa and his sleigh full of gifts quickly across the sky. Do you know the names of Santa's reindeer? They are Comet, Cupid, Dasher, Dancer, Donner, Blitzen, Prancer, and Vixen. Rudolph, the red-nosed reindeer, was not one of Santa's original reindeer.

Christmas angels

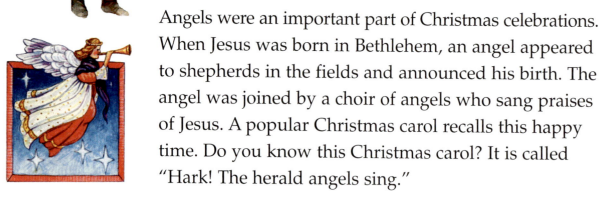

Angels were an important part of Christmas celebrations. When Jesus was born in Bethlehem, an angel appeared to shepherds in the fields and announced his birth. The angel was joined by a choir of angels who sang praises of Jesus. A popular Christmas carol recalls this happy time. Do you know this Christmas carol? It is called "Hark! The herald angels sing."

People believe that angels were at the birth of Jesus.

Some people believe that angels were the Christmas helpers of baby Jesus. As the angels set up the tree, they left behind fine hair that looked like shiny cobwebs. People started putting "angel hair" on Christmas trees. Angel hair was made of spun glass.

25

Christmas dinner

In some homes, Christmas dinner was a huge meal! The family sat at a table loaded with delicious foods. Christmas dishes included roasts such as chicken, turkey, goose, duck, and ham. Potatoes, yams, corn, stuffing, cranberries, and gravy completed the main meal. Then came dessert! Cakes, pies, and candies were all on the table, but everyone's favorite, plum pudding, was brought into the room at the end of the meal. It was covered in flames and made quite a show as it was carried in!

goose

ham

turkey, chicken

Christmas meats included roast chicken, duck, goose, ham, and turkey. Turkeys and chickens were stuffed with dressing and were served with cranberry sauce.

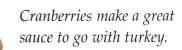

Cranberries make a great sauce to go with turkey.

A Yule log, also called a *Bûche de Noël*, is a chocolate cake rolled up with a filling and frosted to resemble a real holiday Yule log. It was popular with the French settlers.

A plum pudding was prepared five weeks before Christmas, on "Stir-up Sunday." Each family member took a turn stirring the pudding and made a wish while she or he stirred. The pudding was then hung up in a bag. Before it was served, it was boiled for many hours. The pudding was then lit up in flames.

apple and cherry pie

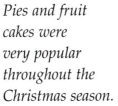

Pies and fruit cakes were very popular throughout the Christmas season.

This fruit cake is called **panettone**.

mince pie

gingerbread cookies

Parties and weddings

By the 1850s, people were able to travel more easily in North America, so family members who lived far away could visit one another. Family reunions made this holiday even more special. During Christmas week, some families held fancy parties in ballrooms that were decorated with garlands, flowers, candles, and Christmas trees.

Christmas weddings

Christmas was the perfect time of the year to be married. Many weddings were held between Christmas and New Year's Day. Homes were already decorated, and family members from other towns often visited. People had free time to enjoy parties and special events such as weddings. It was a great family time!

Ringing in the New Year

New Year's Eve parties allowed people to say goodbye to the old year and celebrate the coming of the new. People found many ways to bring in the new year. They danced away the old year. At midnight, the church bells rang, and people gathered in a circle to sing a song called "Auld Lang Syne." On New Year's Day, young men competed to see who could visit the most young women. They left **calling cards**, or small cards with their names written on them, as proof of their visits.

Mumming was a tradition brought from Europe. Mummers wearing homemade costumes paraded through the streets and visited neighbors. They sang, danced, or performed plays in exchange for food and drinks.

Mumming is still popular in Newfoundland and Philadelphia. In Philadelphia, a mumming parade is held each year on New Year's Day. These costumed mummers were part of a parade in Philadelphia.

Glossary

Note: Many boldfaced words are defined where they appear in the book or are shown by pictures that are labeled.

Advent The four weeks prior to Christmas

calling card A small card with a person's name written on it

cornucopia A horn of plenty filled with fruits, nuts, and candies

cotton batting Layers or sheets of soft cotton used for stuffing furniture or for making crafts

forfeit Something given or taken away as punishment for losing a game

garland A string of vines, flowers, and leaves that are tied together and hung as a decoration

manger An open wooden box that holds food for animals

Martin Luther A German religious leader (1483–1546) whose followers are called Lutherans

mummer A person disguised in a mask or costume

mumming The tradition of wearing costumes and merrymaking

stable A building where farm animals are housed and fed

wreath A decoration of branches and/or flowers that are twisted together into the shape of a circle

Index